rachaelhale

501
THINGS TO FIND

igloobooks

Barlow and Tahlia are attending a special event with their friends.
Can you spot them in the picture opposite?

Barlow

Tahlia

When you've found them, see if you can spot these things, too.

2 mirrors

4 pink bouquets

6 cameras

Pet Show

Now see if you can find
two more furry friends hiding
in each of the other scenes.

Perfect Picnic

Chelsea and Primrose are having a picnic outside. Can you find them in the scene?

Great job!
Can you spot these
things, too?

1 picnic basket

2 melons

5 hot dogs

7 cupcakes

10 bees

15 daisies

Chelsea

Primrose

Beautiful Ballet

Flint and Pebbles are having a
wonderful time at the show.
Can you spot them on the stage?

Bravo!
Now, see you if you can
find these items, too.

1 chandelier

3 harps

6 necklace boxes

This evening's performance is: **Swan Lake**

8 masks

10 bouquets

12 musical notes

Flint

Pebbles

Animal Kingdom

Peanut and Edward are hiding somewhere in their kingdom. Can you spot them in the palace grounds?

Good work! How many of these items can you find?

1 golden fountain

2 toadstools

5 dragonflies

7 crowns

10 caterpillars

15 pink stars

Peanut

Edward

Candyland

Jasmine and Liam are enjoying all the delicious, sweet treats. Can you spot them in this magical land?

Well done. Now, see if you can find these items as well.

1 sweet stall

2 gumball machines

3 ice cream cones

6 heart lollies

8 doughnuts

20 pink sweets

Jasmine

Liam

Classroom Critters

Belle and Sage are top of the class!
Can you see them in the classroom?

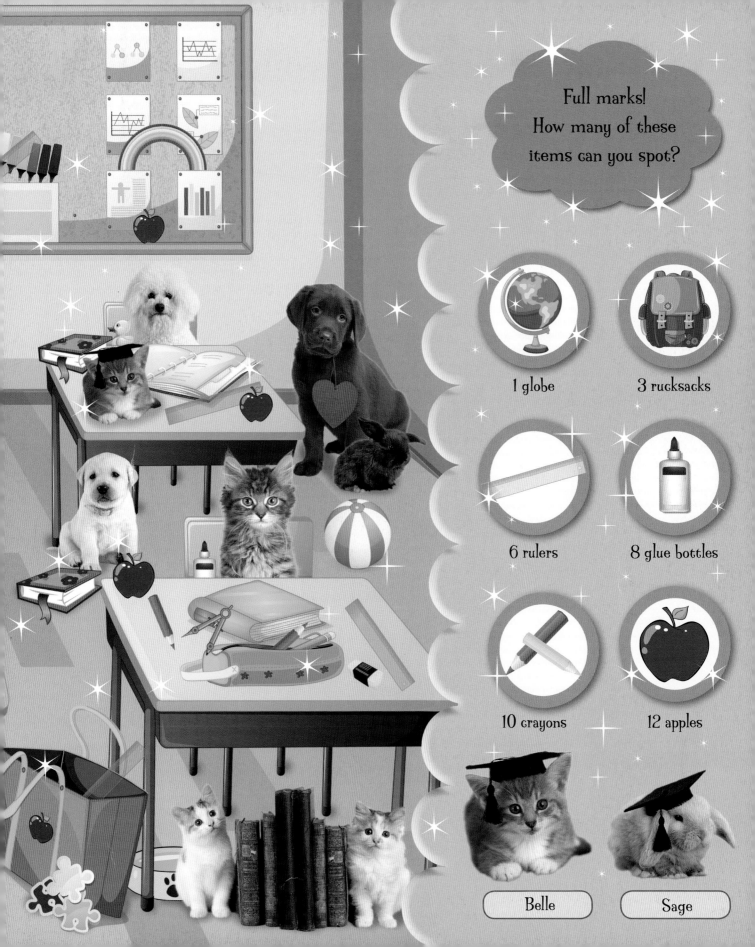

Full marks!
How many of these
items can you spot?

1 globe

3 rucksacks

6 rulers

8 glue bottles

10 crayons

12 apples

Belle

Sage

Farmyard Fun

Henny and Rosie have invited all their friends to play at the farm. Can you find them in the scene?

Well done! Can you spot these items as well?

1 windmill

2 scarecrows

3 hay bales

6 sunflowers

8 caterpillars

20 carrots

Henny

Rosie

Winter Wonderland

Luka and Buddy are wrapped up warm
somewhere in this winter scene.
Can you spot them?

Great job!
Now, see how many
of these items you
can find.

1 postbox

2 snowmen

5 pairs of skis

7 ice skates

10 mittens

15 winter birds

Luka

Buddy

Wonderful Wedding

It's Zenith and Charlie's wedding day!
Can you spot them among the
wedding guests?

Congratulations!
Now, try and find these
things, too.

1 wedding cake

3 ice sculptures

6 wedding bells

8 pink bows

10 diamond rings

12 love hearts

Zenith

Charlie

Party Animals

Willow and Kayla are having a wonderful time at the party. Can you pick them out in the crowd?

Well done!
Can you spot these
things, too?

1 party cake

2 guitars

3 disco balls

6 party horns

8 party hats

20 balloons

Willow

Kayla

Brilliant Bedtime

Lola and Printz are fast asleep after a long day. Can you spot them in the bedroom?

Good work!
Now try and find
these items, too.

1 purple lamp

2 hot chocolates

5 teddy bears

7 storybooks   10 fairies   15 gold stars   Lola   Printz

Congratulations!

Now see if you can find these six items in every picture, too.

If you were looking closely, you'll have spotted everything in the book.

1 collar

1 toy ball

1 water bowl

1 rainbow

1 rubber duck

1 bone

Bonus!

King Geoffrey is hidden somewhere in the book. Can you find him?